The Little Book *of* Heroes

1939-1945

The Little Book *of* Heroes

MARY E. BURKETT

Who are these giants that carry humanity on their shoulders?

ANTON SUKHINSKI

The village idiot

His name was Anton. He lived on the very edge of society in the town of Zborow, Poland – no friends, no family, his home a rundown shack. The townspeople called him the "village idiot."

When the Nazis arrived, they immediately killed 1,000 Jewish men and herded the remaining Jews into a ghetto. Amidst this chaos was the Zeiger family, just a mom and dad with two little boys, and two orphans they were attempting to save. They turned to their former neighbors for help, but could not find one willing soul. That is until they found Anton.

Anton Sukhinski, 1974, with one of the children he saved. Photograph: yadvashem.org

Although physically a very small man, he gladly dug a pit large enough to hold the family of six beneath his shack. The Zeigers would live there with only the light of a small kerosene lamp for nine months. Anton would manage to scavenge enough food to sustain them without drawing the attention of the townspeople and took care of their every need despite the constant threat of Nazi searches and harassment. Zborow was liberated in 1944, and the Zeigers emerged into the sunlight, safe and free once again.

Thirty years later, in 1974, Anton Sukhinski was recognized by Yad Vashem as a Righteous Gentile. He was the only resident of Zborow known to have helped the Jews.

Would I have been as brave, I wonder, as courageous as the "village idiot"?

GENOWEFA MAJCHER

I'll take him!

The year was 1941, the place the Bialystok ghetto in Poland. A baby boy was fighting for his life, his father a freedom fighter and his mother murdered by the Nazis. A young Polish woman named Genowefa Majcher was asked if she would take the baby. Her immediate answer was, "Yes, I'll take him!" She smuggled him out of the ghetto and became his mother. She herself was unmarried and ran a great personal risk if the Nazis found she was harboring a Jewish baby.

Undeterred she gave him a Christian name, Michael, and had him baptized in public. She gave him all the love and care that a mother can give, and on a long-awaited day in 1945, his father returned. Seeing his beautiful son, he knelt down and wept. Michael left with his father, but he stayed in touch with his "Mama" for the rest of her life.

She was recognized as Righteous Among the Nations in 2003 and died the same year. A true heroine.

Genowefa and Michael, 1947. Photograph: jewishmuseummd.org

They refused, simply refused

It was 1942. Norway was in the second year of Nazi occupation with a puppet prime minister in place. New orders arrived – all teachers were to pledge loyalty to the Nazis, join the Nazi national teachers union, and indoctrinate their students accordingly. Parents protested by the thousands, but teachers did something quite remarkable. They refused. Simply refused.

Norwegian teachers imprisoned for refusing to participate in the
Nazi Teachers Association, 1942. Photograph: ushmm.com

The government responded by closing schools and withholding the salaries of 10,000 teachers. Many teachers responded courageously by teaching in their homes. The Nazi retaliation was brutal. Teachers were arrested and sent in freezing cattle cars to concentration camps. Ignoring the danger, Norwegians gathered along the tracks as they passed, singing and offering gifts of food. The teachers were starved, forced to crawl through snow, and endured nighttime marches where they were viciously beaten. Incredibly, months of such treatment did not break their spirits, and they were finally returned to their homes and their newly reopened schools.

What incredible bravery in the face of ultimate evil! Thank you, teachers, for your incredible example! I salute you.

Paper clips

Norwegian students instituted their own silent means of resistance. They used paperclips to make themselves bracelets and necklaces; they wore paperclips in their lapels; they turned their paperclips into a symbol of unity between themselves and their beleaguered teachers. Just imagine, thousands of students speaking eloquently without saying a word! They went even further, turning their backs when Nazi soldiers passed by and singing patriotic Norwegian songs when the Nazis visited their schools.

Students in Oslo high schools refused the compulsory order to join the Nazi Youth Movement and were punished by beatings, threats and arrests. They faced truly grave danger head on. Despite the Nazi brutality, the teenagers simply refused to comply, and eventually the Nazi demands were abandoned. Historians describe the Norwegian resistance as "an unconditional ideological defeat upon Nazism." And just imagine, it started with a bunch of brave kids and their paperclips.

High school students, Oslo, Norway, 1946. Photograph: ushmm.org

Hidden in the handlebars

Gino Bartali was a two-time Tour de France winner – in 1938 and 1948 – an amazing feat to win cycling's greatest prize with a ten-year gap in between, but not his greatest accomplishment. Germany occupied Gino's native Italy in 1943. His fame as a Tour winner allowed him to cycle freely wearing his familiar Italian racing jersey.

Gino Bartali. Photograph: yadvashem.org

He conceived a plan to use his training regimen to aid the Underground. He cycled hundreds of miles throughout much of occupied Italy with counterfeit paperwork hidden in the handlebars and seat of his bike. Gino saved the lives of hundreds of Italian Jews by falsely preventing their deportation to Auschwitz.

Like many heroes after the war, he spoke very little of what he had done. It was only after his death in 2000 that his amazing efforts became known. In 2013, Gino was recognized as Righteous Among the Nations.

Tucked in their coats

In 1940, Hans and Margret were desperate to escape Paris as Nazi tanks rolled in. Having no transportation, Hans assembled bicycles for them from spare parts. Before dawn they dressed warmly and tucked a few possessions in their coats. Amazingly, they bicycled 800 kilometers through France, found the means to sail to Brazil, and eventually reached New York.

Even more amazing was what they tucked inside their coats – the manuscript and sketches for Curious George! The first in the series was published the following year. Thank you, Hans and Margret, for your gift to children around the world!

Hans Augusto and Margret Rey. Photograph: npr.org

And so Paddington Bear was born

They began arriving on a cold day in December of 1938. Eventually almost 10,000 would arrive at the cavernous Reading Station in London. These were the kids of the Kindertransport, little Jewish kids put on trains in Germany by their devastated parents in a desperate effort to save their lives. Each one carried a little suitcase and wore a name tag.

Paddington Bear is a trademark of Paddington and Company.

What a sight this must have been for Londoners –
all those little kids, without their parents, speaking not a
word of English! One of the onlookers would later honor
these brave little folks by writing of a little bear, lost and
alone, wearing a tag saying, "Please look after this bear.
Thanks." And so Paddington Bear was born.

Nowhere to be found

In late September 1943, the Nazis decided to deport the entire Jewish population of Denmark, numbering 7,800 persons. A high-level Nazi attaché, Georg Duckwitz, determined that he could not live with the proposal and informed the Danish resistance. He is credited with a critical decision that saved thousands of lives.

The way in which those lives were saved is quite remarkable. Literally, within three to four days, Danish Jews by the thousands were ferried on fishing vessels across the Oresund from Denmark to Sweden.

How was such a thing accomplished? Knud Dyby was a police officer, a skilled sailor, and an active member of the Danish underground. When he learned of the impending roundup, he used his police access to identify the Nazi patrol routes between Denmark and Sweden.

He took part in planning the massive effort to rescue the Danish Jews. He arranged temporary hiding places in local hospitals and near the fishing docks. He, himself, ferried 1,888 people to safety and also managed five fishing skippers that sailed unceasingly between Denmark and Sweden with weapons, intelligence, news and fleeing Jews. When the Nazi round up began on October 1, it was quickly deemed a failed campaign and called off, because 7,220 of the 7,800 Danish Jews were nowhere to be found.

Denmark was liberated in May 1945, and the following year, Knud moved to the United States. He died in September 2011 at the age of 96, an unsung hero. Thank you, sir.

Danish fishermen ferry Jews to
safety. Photograph: ushmm.org

Knud Dyby. Photograph: jfr.org

ROZA

Little Rose

In 1943, the Warsaw Uprising was crushed by the Nazis. The military action by the Polish Home Army had lasted 63 days. In a heroic effort to free Warsaw from Nazi rule, 2,500 partisans took on 25,000 German soldiers equipped with tanks, artillery and heavy weaponry. Only one quarter of the partisans had weapons of any kind, many only pistols. The end result? The Nazis razed Warsaw to the ground and 180,000 civilians were murdered in retaliation. Eleven hundred partisans were captured and deported.

Roza Maria Gozdziewska. Photograph: Eugeniusz Lokajski warsawinstitute.org

In the midst of this chaos and horror was a little girl, eight-year-old Roza. Her father had been killed by the Gestapo in 1943, and Roza had escaped her burning home with her older sister, Zofia, during the Uprising. She found refuge in a basement field hospital where she became the youngest nurse in the Polish Resistance. As she provided sips of water and encouraged her patients with smiles and good cheer, they nicknamed her "Little Rose."

Roza survived the war, later graduated from college, and moved to France, where she died in 1989. Her iconic photo, by Resistance photographer, Eugeniusz Lokajski, illustrates that courage comes in all shapes and sizes. Thank you, Little Rose, for your marvelous example to us all!

I know what I am fighting for

He would not see his 40th birthday, but even so Father Franz Reinisch could not do the unthinkable. He could not swear allegiance to the Fuhrer, nor could he serve in the German army. "You cannot take an oath to a criminal. You cannot follow an authority that brings only murder and death into the world," he told his friends.

Franz Reinisch became a priest at age 25 and in the years that followed became a popular Christian speaker throughout Germany. In the 1930s, Franz spoke out bravely as he watched both Hitler and hatred grow in power. He held the simple belief that Nazism and Christianity were incompatible. Of course, his stance would draw the attention of the Gestapo, and he was banned from public speaking.

On April 15, 1942, Father Franz was ordered to report for induction into the military. He boldly stated that he would swear allegiance only to the German people and was immediately arrested, tried and five days later sentenced to death. In his statement to the court, Father Franz said, "I am a Catholic priest with only the weapons of the Holy Spirit and the Faith; but I know what I am fighting for." He was beheaded at 3:30 a.m. the following morning.

Franz Reinisch. Photograph: offerta.roma-belmonte.info

They stood

They wore their hair long because the Hitler Youth wore theirs short. They wore traditional German attire, refusing the dreaded brown shirts. They irritated the Nazis in countless small ways, pouring sugar into gas tanks and stealing bicycles. They simply weren't buying what the National Socialists were selling – the vision of a totalitarian Utopia was not for them. They were German teens who stood against the greatest evil of the 20th century. They left school at age 14 to avoid mandatory participation in the Hitler Youth. At age 18, they would be forced into compulsory military service, but in those three years, they stood. They scribbled graffiti, protected Jews, delivered explosives to resisters.

The Edelweiss Pirates. Photograph: facinghistory.org

Who were these incredible kids? They gave themselves a name – the Edelweiss Pirates. Many would pay a price of course. At the least, their heads were shaved. At worst, they were beaten, imprisoned, tortured, and on the morning of November 10, 1944 in Cologne, six of the them were publicly hanged without trial. And remember, these were kids, the high school students of today. One can anticipate bravery among grown men and women, but this? Heroism is indeed found in the most unexpected places. I salute you.

The best that I could do

She was 11 when the Nazis came to power, and like most German kids, she was enthralled with the youthful camaraderie they offered. She joined the BDM, the League of German Girls, and steadily advanced in its ranks. Her older brother, Hans, however, and several of her siblings were members of the White Rose, a non-Nazi youth group. Although initially allowed, such alternative groups were eventually banned in 1936, and her siblings were arrested for continuing their activities. Their arrests awakened in Sophie a recognition of injustice that in time would transform her into an intrepid anti-Nazi resistance fighter.

By June of 1942, Germany was in its third year of war, and Sophie and Hans found themselves together at the University of Munich. Hans, a medical student, was already involved in the White Rose anti-Nazi movement, and as soon as Sophie discovered his secret, she insisted on joining him. Over the next seven months they, and a handful of fellow students, would produce six widely distributed pamphlets of a heroic nature we can hardly imagine today.

"Our current 'state' is the dictatorship of evil... I ask you, if you know that, then why don't you act?"

"The German name will remain forever tarnished unless finally the German youth stands up... Students! The German people look to us! The responsibility is ours..."

Sophie, Hans, and Christoph Probst were caught distributing pamphlets and arrested on February 18, 1943. In the half-day trial that followed, Sophie made this statement: "I am, now as before, of the opinion that I did the best that I could do for my nation." Sophie and her co-defendants were found guilty and beheaded by guillotine four days later. Their three friends, Willi Graf, Alexander Schmorell, and Kurt Huber were arrested days later and put to death. Sophie Scholl was 21 years old.

Sophie Scholl. Photograph: nationalww2museum.org

What's in a name?

The boys, Hermann and Albert, just two years apart in age, grew up in the castle of Veldenstein near Nurnberg, Germany. Ironically, as it would turn out, the castle was owned by their mother's lover, Ritter von Epenstein, a Jew. Hermann, the older of the boys, was loud, brash and outgoing. Albert was the quiet one, introspective, a reader. They could not have been more different.

Hermann was 19 when he joined the fledging German Air Force as WWI began. In another 20 years he would be infamous as Germany's top military commander, founder of the Gestapo, and Hitler's right-hand man – Hermann Goering.

Albert Goering. Photograph: timesofisrael.com

Albert Goering, on the other hand, hated Nazism and moved to Vienna, but in the years that followed, he found his well-known name quite useful. He saved his Jewish friends and complete strangers by simply forging papers and signing his brother's name. He even sent trucks to concentration camps with orders for "workers" and then sent them to forests where the prisoners were released.

After the war, however, his name would haunt him. He was imprisoned as a potential war criminal for 15 months and only released on the testimony of 34 Jews whom he had saved. Even so, he could find no one who would hire a man with the hated Goering name. He lived the remainder of his life an alcoholic subsisting on a small government pension. But until his death in 1966, the food packages never stopped arriving, gifts from those he had saved, those who called his name blessed.

A wave of opportunity

She wasn't supposed to be there of course. There were 160,000 men landing on the beaches that day. She was meant to be in relative safety, sitting on a transport barge in the English Channel with all the other journalists. But the previous evening, Martha Gellhorn had boldly boarded a hospital barge with her press credentials and the story that she was there to interview nurses. It was a sham, of course, but it got her on board, where she found a bathroom and locked herself in. She spent a miserable night, horribly seasick, but when she crept out of her hiding place the next morning, she had a front-row seat to one of history's greatest moments – the invasion of Normandy on June 6, 1944.

Thousands of ships faced the great cliffs as tons of bombs rained from overhead. It would be perhaps the greatest news story of all time, but Martha found that it wasn't her skill as a writer that was needed. The sea was filled with dead and wounded soldiers, and she leapt into action, helping wherever and however she could. At nightfall, she waded ashore with the medics and found herself on Omaha Beach, a stretcher-bearer with blistered hands, soaked to the skin with sea water and exhaustion. She would labor through the night, the daring she had known the night before transformed into bravery as she followed the mine sweepers. Martha Gellhorn would leave that place in the days to come a different person, no longer an observer of history, but a participant – the lone woman in the D-Day invasion.

Martha Gellhorn. Photograph: Lee Miller townandcountrymag.com

We are all Jews

They didn't expect to find themselves POWs in German Stalag IX-A. They had fought their way through the freezing Ardennes Forest over the Christmas of 1944, but ultimately were captured by the Nazis. And so on that fateful morning, U.S. Army Master Sergeant Roddie Edmonds and a thousand of his men stood at attention before the camp commander. Master Sergeant Edmonds had been ordered to identify the Jewish soldiers among his troops, and he had no doubt of their fates if he did so.

"We are all Jews here," he replied. The commander furiously pointed his pistol at the sergeant. "They cannot all be Jews!" Even in the face of death, he did not waver. "We are all Jews," he repeated. "According to the Geneva Convention, we have to give only our name, rank, and serial number. If you shoot me, you'll have to shoot all of us and after the war, you'll be tried for war crimes."

Master Sergeant Roddie Edmonds. Photograph: yadvashem.org

Four months later, when the camp was liberated, the 200 Jewish men under Master Sergeant Edmonds' command walked out of Stalag IX-A with their comrades. Sergeant Edmonds died in 1985, never having told of his heroism on that freezing day 40 years before.

After his death, his children began reading his wartime diary and unearthed the story of their father's incredible bravery. Twenty-six thousand people have been honored as Righteous Among the Nations for their heroic efforts to save Jewish lives during the Holocaust. Master Sergeant Roddie Edmonds is the lone U.S. serviceman so honored.

They remembered who they once were

It began in 1685. The king of France forbade French Huguenots to leave France and had them ruthlessly hunted down. A half million French citizens would die, but many would hide to escape persecution. In South Central France, the village of Le Chambon became riddled with secret rooms and secret paths leading to freedom in Switzerland. These rooms and paths would be kept secret... just in case they were ever needed again.

In the bitter cold winter of 1940, a Jewish woman, fleeing persecution, knocked on the door of Pastor André Trocmé in Le Chambon. The pastor and his wife offered shelter and asked the mayor for help in securing false papers for her. He refused, and the pastor turned instead to his congregation, saying, "I do not know what a Jew is. I only know human beings." They swiftly set up a travel network. By what means? Oh yes, the well-kept secret of centuries past. There were only 5,000 villagers in Le Chambon, but they managed to save 5,000 Jews. You see, they remembered who they once were and knew who they now wanted to be. Thank you, brave heroes.

Children sheltered in Le Chambon. Photograph: ushmm.org

Keepers of promises

It was simple really. They lived by Besa, the highest ethical code in Albania. It means to be a person to whom one can entrust one's life and one's family, a keeper of promises. Albania was first annexed by Italy in WWII and then by the Germans. The resistance to the occupiers was fierce and complex, but far-removed from poor farmers like Destan and Lime Balla.

In 1943, at the time of Ramadan, 17 Jews fleeing the Nazis came to their tiny village of Shengjergji. The three Lazar brothers were sheltered by Destan and Lime, and the others were divided among their Muslim neighbors. They were dressed as farmers and kept safe for 15 months before being rescued by partisans – even the local police knew of their identities.

Lime Balla. Photograph: yadvashem.org

Despite the villagers' deep poverty, they neither asked for nor expected payment for their kindness. As I said, it was simple. "All of us villagers were Muslims. We were sheltering God's children under our Besa." Almost all Jews living within Albania, both native and refugee, were saved, and in fact, there were more Jews in Albania at the end of the war than before it began. For the Lazar brothers, this simple code, this Besa, was the difference between life and death. Destan and Lime Balla were recognized as Righteous Among the Nations in 1992.

The difference between right and wrong

In 1942, Belgium was experiencing its second year of brutal occupation by the Nazis. Jeanne Daman was a teacher in Brussels and a Catholic, who had never met a Jewish person in her young life. She was surrounded, however, by the example of nuns in convents across Belgium who were actively hiding as many Jewish children as possible.

When Jewish children were no longer allowed to attend public kindergartens, Jeanne accepted a position as head mistress of Nos Petits, a private school for Jewish students, numbering about 325 children. Every school day, however, two dramatic changes were noted: some children simply disappeared as their families were rounded up for deportation, while others were instantly orphaned when their parents were arrested during school hours. Imagine how unbelievable and terrifying this must have seemed to their young teacher!

It became clear that desperate efforts were needed to save the children. Jeanne became part of a network which placed Jewish mothers in Belgian homes as maids and also placed orphaned children in private homes. As the children were so young, they could not be sent alone, and Jeanne traveled all over Belgium accompanying them to new homes.

Eventually, she assumed a false identity and became a social worker for a German welfare organization, Secours d'Hiver. In this role she was able to carry out illegal operations and even to transport arms. By the end of the war, she had worked clandestinely with two underground organizations, the Mouvement Royal Belge and the Armee Belge des Partisans. When the war ended, she helped young Jewish children to be reunited with their families before she moved to the U.S. in 1946.

In 1971, Jeanne was recognized as Righteous Among the Nations and in 1980 was awarded the Entr'aide Medal under the patronage of the King of Belgium. Where did Jeanne find the bravery for her intrepid deeds? She simply said she had been taught the difference between "right and wrong."

Jeanne Daman. Photograph: ushmm.org

He took an oath

It was July 15, 1942, a hot day during a hot week in Paris. Theo Larue found out that a roundup of Jews was scheduled for the next day. He immediately alerted the eight Jewish families in his building and set to work getting false papers for his neighbors, the Lictensztajns. Theo's information was correct. The following day, the French police, on orders of the Nazi occupiers, rounded up 7,000 Jews, 4,000 of whom were children, and held them in an indoor bicycle stadium, the Velodrome d'Hiver. They were held for five days in the searingly hot stadium with no food, no water, no sanitation and then shipped to various internment camps.

Theophile Larue. Photograph: ushmm.org

The Lictensztajns, however, were not among those in the Vel d'Hiv or on one of those trains because Theo had successfully secreted them away to the south of France with his false papers. What makes this story remarkable lies in one small detail – Theo Larue wasn't a shopkeeper, or a clerk, or an artist. He was a Parisian policeman, one of the very men entrusted with rounding up the Jews. Why did he do it? Why did he risk his own life and his family's? Well, simply put, he had taken an oath, and that oath charged him with protecting all citizens, so he did.

Theophile Larue and his wife, Madeleine, were recognized as Righteous Among the Nations in 2007.

Dancing with death

Dorothy Baggett was 21 years old on March 1, 1942, when she graduated from St. Margaret's Nursing School in Montgomery, Alabama. How could she have imagined that three short years later, she would enter the gates of the Dachau Concentration Camp as one of 80 nurses of the U.S. Army Nurse Corps, 127th Evacuation Hospital?

Arriving just three days after liberation, what she and her fellow nurses encountered almost defied description. Bodies were piled everywhere. The living were starving, dehydrated and ravaged with disease, including typhus. Two thousand cases were diagnosed in the first four days alone, and 80 percent of the former prisoners had tuberculosis.

Incredibly, within 36 hours, these 80 nurses, assisted by clergy and corpsmen, had two hospitals up and running. For the next four months they, along with German nurses pressed into service and reinforcements from other hospital units, would care for thousands of the desperately ill. With constant and intensive care, many slowly recovered, but countless others were simply too weak or too ill to survive. Captain Wahlstrom of the Nurse Corps said, "We felt we were dancing with death. We couldn't get away from it and wondered if it would ever stop."

Heroism comes in many forms and often at high personal cost. I honor the memory of these brave young women, far from home, who gave their all in circumstances we can scarcely imagine.

Dorothy Baggett. Photograph: ww2veteranshistoryproject.com

Willingly and voluntarily

June 15, 1941 – "Dear Mama, At the end of the month of May I was transferred to the camp of Auschwitz. Everything is well in my regard. Be tranquil about me and about my health, because the good God is everywhere and provides for everything with love."

These words were written by Father Maximilian Kolbe, a Polish Catholic priest and Franciscan friar. During the German occupation of Poland, he remained at Niepokalanów, a monastery that housed 650 friars. Many Polish refugees and Jews sought sanctuary in the monastery, and Father Kolbe and the Franciscan community helped to hide, feed and clothe 3,000 souls. On February 17, 1941, the Gestapo invaded the monastery and arrested Father Kolbe for hiding Jews. He was interned briefly in a Polish prison and then sent to Auschwitz, where he was branded prisoner #16670. His mama was undoubtedly frantic for his safety until finally in the summer, she received his words of reassurance.

It was just a month later when three prisoners appeared to have escaped from the Auschwitz. As punishment, the Deputy Commander ordered 10 men to be chosen to be starved to death in an underground bunker. When one of the men, Franciszek Gajowniczek, heard he was selected, he cried out "My wife! My children!" And it was at this moment, Father Kolbe spoke up. "What does this Polish pig want?" the Nazi commander asked. Father Kolbe repeated himself, pointing to the condemned Franciszek Gajowniczek saying, "I am a Catholic priest from Poland. I would like to take his place because he has a wife and children." Contemptuously, the commander accepted Kolbe, unconcerned with which of them lived or died.

Gajowniczek later said: "I could only thank him with my eyes. I was stunned and could hardly grasp what was going on. The immensity of it: I, the condemned, am to live and someone else willingly and voluntarily offers his life for me – a stranger. Is this some dream? I was

Maximilian Kolbe. Photograph: saintmaximiliankolbe.co/

put back into my place without having had time to say anything to Maximilian Kolbe. I was saved. And I owe to him the fact that I could tell you all this. The news quickly spread all round the camp. It was the first and the last time that such an incident happened in the whole history of Auschwitz."

Father Kolbe never asked for anything and did not complain. He led the starving prisoners in prayer and singing of hymns. After two weeks, most of the prisoners were dead, but Father Kolbe remained kneeling in the center of the cell. One of the SS guards remarked, "This priest is really a great man. We have never seen anyone like him..." Ultimately the SS guards were ordered to empty the cell. It was said that Father Kolbe offered his arm without protest and received the lethal injection that ended his life. It was early August, 1941, just six weeks or so since he wrote his last words to his mother.

Father Maximilian Kolbe was canonized as a Confessor of the Faith and ultimately as a saint of the

Catholic Church in 1981. Many honored guests and notaries were present at his canonization, and among them sat a man with a unique story – Franciszek Gajowniczek, a man who miraculously survived Auschwitz to tell the world of Maximilian Kolbe.

ABOUT THE AUTHOR

Mary Burkett is a Holocaust educator with a truly unique and innovative approach to education for both students and the general public. Mary draws fine art portraits of children killed in the Holocaust and writes brief stories of heroism and bravery during the Holocaust/WWII era. This dynamic combination attracts one to two million views from around the world each month on social media. She partners with Anne Frank USA, the Butterfly Project in San Diego, and other organizations for exhibits and lectures. Her portraits have been used for Yom HaShoah in the Israeli Embassies in Paris and Washington, D.C., been recognized by the U.S. House of Representatives, and been praised by the White House and the Dean of Canterbury Cathedral, among many others. The documentary film *Beloved Children of the Holocaust* was completed in 2022. Mary's ultimate goal is to teach the importance of human equality and the sacredness of each individual human life.

View all of Mary's collections:
maryburkettart.com

Read Mary's new story weekly:
facebook.com/maryburkettbeloved

Learn more about the film:
belovedchildrenoftheholocaust.com

24278382R00053